How to look after your Human

How to look after your Human

Milly & Zara Lorimer

Spiral Bound Publishing

First published in 2013
Copyright © 2013, David Lorimer
Cover design: Charlotte Lorimer
All rights reserved.
ISBN - 978-1-291-22146-6
Contact: David Lorimer, Gibliston Mill, Colinsburgh, Leven, Fife KY9 1JS, Scotland.
www.lookafteryourhuman.com
www.facebook.com/lookafteryourhuman
www.twitter.com/lookafterhumans
www.instagram.com/lookafteryourhuman

Contents

Introduction...1
Who we are..5
How to make your Humans feel welcome....11
How to communicate with your Humans.....16
How to de-stress your Humans.................20
How to keep your Humans healthy.............33
How to keep your Humans clean................46
How to help your Humans around the house and garden....................................49
How to apologise for occasional mistakes....53
How to pose for photos...........................62

Introduction

Humans have a strange idea that they look after their dogs. The truth is quite different: we actually look after them. And as life becomes more and more stressful for humans, they need more and more looking after. In this book we are going to give other dogs a few tips about how best to do this.

Humans seem to rush around at great speed doing all sorts of urgent tasks while we take life at a much more relaxed pace, as we always have. We think humans have a thing or two to learn from us dogs.

Of course we love excitement - but too much excitement all the time just wears you out. Besides, the rhythm of life is activity followed by rest - we dogs sleep for up to 18 hours a day. Far too many are stressed humans out and we think it's our job to try to help them slow down a bit and get life in proportion.

We dogs learn from an early age that life is all about love. The more love you give your human, the more love you will receive in return. It's a very simple philosophy, but it's practical and effective. And it makes both humans and dogs happy.

Who we are

Hello! My name is Milly and my daughter is called Zara. We are two black Labradors living in the countryside in Fife in Scotland. I was born on 4th March 2006 and Zara was born on 15th June 2009. We were both born at home so we have been looking after our humans all our lives!

We have four humans to look after, but sometimes George is away at school for quite a long time. But when he is here we normally have to help him get out of bed in the morning. Teenagers huh? Charlotte doesn't need waking up and takes us out for runs or cycle rides in the morning, which we love. Then there is Jane (Charlotte and George's mum) who often needs my special stress-reduction cuddles on the sofa. Finally there is David who is always looking out for us, cuddling us and taking us for lots of runs.

Our humans are always comparing me with Zara. They say that I'm very graceful and composed while Zara is far more enthusiastic and boisterous. We look quite different too. I am slim and sleek while Zara is more chunky, taking after her father. I'm a better runner while I have to admit that Zara is a better swimmer.

Zara is the fourth generation of our Labrador family. When Jane, David and Charlotte came to visit Islay, Zara's great grandmother, she knew that she had to go home with them, especially as baby Charlotte needed a playmate! Islay had a litter of four and Flora stayed on to have Milly, one of six, who then had Zara, also one of six.

David used to live in the big house, opposite the

house we are living in now, which he and Jane converted from stables. He also grew up with Labradors. One of them, Juno, lived to 14 and once had a litter of 14 – that must have been exhausting!

I was shocked to discover that previous Family Labradors in the 1950s and 1960s lived outside in a kennel and slept on straw. I can't imagine what their humans were thinking, as we live in our lovely warm kitchen. The only time we ever slept outside was when we were puppies and we were making too much mess to be allowed inside!

We are very lucky. Not only do we have our own beds on the floor, but we have also taken over the kitchen sofa (along with most of the other sofas in the house.) Our humans appreciate our kitchen sofa cuddles and kindly bought us a special tartan rug. Although, they find that they need to renew it twice a year as somehow holes appear in it...we can't think how.

We also encountered a similar problem with our old beanbag beds. The beans kept on coming out and they became more and more uncomfortable - terrible! They were supposed to be guaranteed for 10 years, but I don't think they lasted more than two!

We live a simple life - sleep, walks, food, cuddles - and sitting by the log fire under a table (or better still on a sofa) in the evening. We are happy dogs and make others happy - what more can we ask from life?

How to make your humans feel welcome

It's very important that your humans appreciate how much you love them. Every day should start with lots of wagging - the aim is to make them smile!

They don't often match our enthusiasm first thing in the morning but we don't take it personally - they just haven't woken up properly (especially George – he's like a zombie until lunchtime!)

It's vital that you continue to greet your humans enthusiastically throughout the day. We always show our delight at being with them by frantically wagging our tails, even if they have only been away for a few minutes.

In the evening, when you are already sitting comfortably on a sofa or under a table, you can save energy by simply wagging your tail when your human comes in - no need to get up.

We're even more excited to see our humans again after they have been on a long trip. David is often away for a few days and George can be away at school for weeks at a time!

It's important to give them a really good welcome home. We wag our tails wildly and they don't mind if we jump up a little bit. Then they often come into the kitchen and sit down with us on the sofa.

David's friend Rupert Sheldrake has done lots of experiments with telepathic dogs who know their owners are coming home. It's all written down in *Dogs That Know Their Owners are Coming Home* if you want to know more.

No one has ever done the experiment with us, but of course it would work. We would just need to tune in.

David's mother had a dog just like us called Duschka when she was a girl many years ago. She left Duschka with a farmer neighbour and went off to Edinburgh. She didn't come back for some weeks, but when she got back, Duschka was waiting to welcome her on the front steps of her house!

We're also very good at making our humans' guests feel welcome, after we have barked hello, that is. I feel that it is only polite to go round to each guest in turn and give them a cuddle. However, when there are lots of people I do find this a bit exhausting. I could only manage half of our summer drinks party – it was a bit of a tall order!

We greet humans and dogs differently. It is polite for dogs to approach from the side, tails up and have a good sniff. Humans may think this looks a bit rude, but for us smelling is very important.

How to communicate with your Humans

As you dogs know, humans are not very observant. We dogs actually study them all the time, monitoring the slightest movements of their body language. If they take the trouble to look at us closely, they will see our ears pricked up and moving, eyes alert and face twitching in anticipation.

We understand some human language but most of all, we understand tone of voice - the way things are said rather than what people say. Even human research shows that their tone of voice is much more important than what they actually say.

Most of the time when we yawn, we're tired just like our humans, and yawning sends oxygen to our brain. But we also yawn if we're stressed or our humans have just scolded us – most humans don't know this.

We use our ears a lot to send messages. We prick up our ears when we are interested in something and wiggle them about. If we're puzzled we might tilt our head to the side and even frown. We also move our eyebrows and nose, just like humans.

Our eyes face forward, while some animals like rabbits have eyes on the side so they can see us coming. This doesn't make much difference as we usually catch up with them anyway, unless they annoyingly go down a small hole we can't get into ourselves.

We find humans staring directly at us a bit threatening, so if they do this we're likely to turn away.

Sometimes we dogs try staring to influence our humans. We stare at them, then at their food. This means that we'd like some, but it doesn't usually work. I tried this recently at breakfast by staring at David then at his piece of toast. No deal. (If he gave me some, that would be a submissive gesture, and I'd just try it again.)

Directing your gaze specifically is also useful when you want some water. You just go over to the empty bowl when your human is in the kitchen and look at it intently. Then you look up at them, and down again at the bowl. They usually get the message and fill the bowl up.

Sitting down patiently and looking expectant is a good way to communicate that you are ready for food. It does usually hurry them up and then they will say 'good girl', pat you and put the bowl straight down. It's simple, really.

How to de-stress your humans

As we mentioned earlier, humans need a lot of looking after, especially as their lives become more stressed. Many humans overwork in what they call the 'fast lane'. We think they need to spend more time in the slow lane. My main way of helping humans unwind is to sit quietly with them on the sofa while preventing them from getting up.

Being able to sit on comfortable sofas and chairs is important as cuddles on sofas are by far the best way to de-stress your humans. Luckily, our humans appreciate this. We have several cuddle allocated sofas.

The real challenge is when a new sofa arrives.

It's OK to climb onto an old sofa, but new sofas are definitely OFF LIMITS! 'No dogs on the new sofa', they said.

Actually, it's only a matter of time before your humans get used to you being on the new sofa. You can always try it out when your human is in another part of the house then look surprised if they come in and find you lying on it.

"Milly, WHAT ARE YOU DOING ON THE NEW SOFA?"

"What, me?"

"I'm just minding my own business."

The best thing is to get down, immediately and quickly, and head for an older sofa in another room. These old sofas can be more comfortable. And you can always try again later.

When the humans are actually sitting on the new sofa, you can approach with an appealing look and put one paw up, then the other. "Down, Milly, this sofa is not for dogs."

At least, not yet. Just go back under the table for the time being. Looking after the new sofa can create temporary stress for your humans who can become very selfish on the arrival of the new sofa. However, perseverance pays off in the end and both of you will be happier with the extra cuddles!

Our humans have remained strict about not being allowed on beds, though. We are not allowed on ANY beds, except for stockings on Christmas morning, when we have a special permit. When I was doing some research, I found that more than half the dogs in Britain

sleep on their human's bed. We don't think this is a very good idea as humans move around so much that it would prevent us sleeping. After all, we need a lot more sleep than they do. Looking after them is exhausting!

Now, back to those cuddle treatment instructions.

One of my special tricks is to approach a human from behind and put my head between their knees – this almost guarantees a nice stroke and may encourage them to move to a sofa.

Once the human has sat down on the sofa, I get up beside them and put my head and paws on their lap. I signal the start of the treatment by letting out a gentle sigh and half-closing my eyes.

The effectiveness of this treatment can be enhanced in the evening with a relaxing glass of wine - this sometimes causes the human to sigh contentedly as well.

Visitors may need a special induction session. They can opt into this just by sitting down on the kitchen sofa.

I also conduct special stress-management sessions for Jane on the library sofa. This is a smaller sofa that can just fit two humans and a dog, or two dogs. I have to wait until Jane has finished her food before starting the treatment. If I try to climb up while she is still eating, this can increase her (and my) stress levels.

The great thing about my treatments is that I get to relax at the same time! I love being stroked, especially behind my ears.

Sometimes Zara ends my treatments suddenly by getting onto the same sofa, normally right on top of the person I am treating. Her idea of helping people is trying to get them excited, which is the opposite of mine. She turns upside down, grunts and wriggles about, which can unsettle both me and the human. Or else she licks them enthusiastically, which is lovely but not very peaceful and does make humans laugh! In fact just looking at Zara's expressions can make them laugh.

Not only can we dogs de-stress our humans, we can also help by removing some sources of stress. We think that every effort should be made to reduce the time they spend on technology as it seems to increase their stress levels considerably.

For example, we don't think checking emails is a good way for our humans to start the day – much better to go for a walk. So if your human is doing their emails at breakfast, climb up sideways on and give them a little nudge and a lick. This is not always appreciated and sometimes we are pushed away and told to get down, but don't be disheartened. Keep at it!

Chewing chargers, TV remotes, important cables, headphones etc. is also a fantastic way to prevent humans using technology. However, this can be stressful in the short term, as you are likely to be told off and shouted at by your human, who does not realise that you have their best interests at heart.

For us, chewing is a form of stress management, but most humans don't seem to know this. Chewing things can go badly wrong, though, and we get into trouble, which is very stressful for us as well as our humans. We will give you some tips later on about how to apologise for this kind of thing.

Human scientists talk about how humans feel better when they look after other people or pets. So humans feeding us, taking us for walks and giving us cuddles makes us both happy!

We dogs don't need very much: water, food, shelter, exercise and love.

Food should always be a matter of routine. We get fish or sardines for breakfast. Sardines are my one beauty product - they keep my coat sleek and shiny, and they're yummy! I like the ones with tomato sauce. When we were puppies we got carrots and eggs as well - we still love catching and crunching carrots when George throws them for us.

Our other meal is after our afternoon run. We have our humans well trained as they pretty much stick to this routine. However, it is sometimes tricky to get them to keep to their afternoon walk schedule.

Taking your human for a walk is also a good way to get them to wind down and is an important part of keeping your human healthy too! So that's what we'll talk about next.

How to keep your humans healthy

Humans need exercise to stay healthy, so getting them out for walks is very important and a good way of looking after them. It suits us too, as we just love walks, or rather runs - we go a lot further and faster than they do!

We have our first walk after breakfast, or that's the theory. At weekends, though, things can get badly delayed as our humans tend to get up later, which is pretty inconvenient for us. We just have to hang around. It also means that our breakfast is late.

It's important to give your human very clear signals that they need to go for a walk. The main thing is to show them that you are all

ready to go for a walk so they can get their act together.

It takes us no time at all to get ready, we don't even need leads where we live, but humans seem to have put on all sorts of stuff - coats, hats and wellies - before they go outside. Then sometimes they even go to the bathroom just as you thought they were going out. This causes a further delay.

One way of emphasising your message is by doing what humans call 'the downward dog.' I think that humans imitate this movement in Yoga, a strange form of exercise, but I'm sure they don't do it us well as us. You stretch forward and down on your front legs arching your back - you can also make a friendly sound to add to the effect.

Another effective tactic is vigorously shaking your head and ears, making it quite clear that

you're ready to go, even if they aren't. It does hurry them up.

Even when we are already outside waiting, our humans can still be rather slow and may need further encouragement. You can sit down on the grass and wag your tail horizontally along the ground while looking attentively at your human.

While on the walk it is important to come back occasionally to check if your humans are keeping up with your pace. Don't let them look at the view for too long – you've got to keep their heart rate up!

Humans are very visual and they don't realise how many interesting smells there are on our walks. We sniff intently to gather information - smell is our top sense. In fact, we can smell things at 100 million times lower concentration than humans can! No wonder life is so interesting. Some of us are even used for tracking or to help the police.

Humans don't know that we have pretty good sight as well and that we can identify our human in a group up to a mile away!

We also have very acute hearing. We can hear cars well before humans. Our ears enable us to pinpoint the location of any sound. We can hear four times the distance of humans.

After we have taken our humans back home, we quite often spend the day in David's office. In the morning, we sleep. We have no idea what he does there or why it takes so long. We hope that occasional cuddles help.

Being in the office means that we can keep him on schedule for his afternoon walk. When you think your human has done enough work, just climb up sideways if they are at a desk or get

onto the sofa or chair if they are reading. Put your nose under the book or paper and give it a firm nudge. It works every time.

From time to time we jump into the back of the car to go for our walk. This is very exciting. Our favourite places are Elie Golf Course and the West Sands at St Andrews. At Elie there are people hitting a small white ball with sticks then striding off after them – very odd. I gather that we are not meant to pick these balls up, although we do know a spaniel, Hector, who finds lots of these balls in all sorts of places. His human seems very pleased, but we have never found one.

Before we go on the West Sands, we often have to spend rather a long time in the back of the car. David comes and gets things from the car, but it can take him ages before he is ready for a run.

We LOVE the West Sands. It goes on for miles and apparently some famous human runners have trained and made a film there. We usually go along one side of the dunes then across and back on the sand. If the tide is in, we go straight into the sea.

We often meet other interesting dogs. Just the other day we saw a Dalmatian open the back window of a jeep with her nose and start barking at us - so naturally we all had a good bark!

Occasionally it snows. It's still important to get your humans outside and we can help them go sledging on the hill. This is so much fun! You can chase your humans down the hill on a sledge and see if you can knock them off before they get to the bottom!

Diet is also a very important aspect of keeping your humans healthy. For example, cake is not very good for humans so you can help them out by eating some. Humans may assume that the cake is out of reach, but not for a hungry dog.

Just recently we were up in Glen Lyon and one of our humans left three-quarters of a nice Victoria sponge on a shelf in the larder overnight, which gave us plenty of time to finish it off. I always tell Zara that she shouldn't eat cake but it's irresistible and I usually end up by joining in. In fact I had so much that I couldn't eat my breakfast (of course she managed hers).

Luckily our other human didn't realise what had been in the empty plastic bag in the morning, but all was revealed at teatime when it was discovered that the cake was MISSING!

We have noticed that humans tend to eat far too much food at BBQs. We are happy to help them out by eating some but we often find BBQs infuriating as the smell of roasting meat is delicious, but then we rarely get any as our humans are on the lookout.

However, unexpected opportunities for extra food may arise.

Step 1: pick your moment to approach the other food, while your human is guarding the meat.

Step 2: nonchalantly ease your way towards the nice crispy roll while your human is telling a joke.

Step 3: keeping your eyes on your human, slowly approach the roll and take it gently in your mouth.

Step 4: turn your back to your human and eat the roll, making as little noise as possible.
Step 5: check you have no roll on the side of your mouth and approach your human, wagging your tail as if nothing has happened.

Zara only got to Step 3 when my human caught her in the act - even the small nibble was worth it, though!

How to keep your humans clean

Taking your humans for a swim is a good way to keep them clean.

Our favourite beach in England is Aldeburgh. We go there every summer. This gives us a chance to get our humans into the sea in the mornings, which is also good exercise for them. We also love looking after our host Janine, who swims even better than we do.

Humans may also need another swim in the afternoon, especially if they have been playing tennis. Zara just adores swimming and can't wait to get our humans into the water. She then swims alongside them to give them encouragement. She will even try to retrieve stones from rivers...

When we've had enough, we let them know by having a good shake. This feels great but some reason, if we get too close to them, they jump away and shriek. Zara thinks this is very funny and I'm sure she gets extra muddy on purpose to add to the effect.

We don't mind how wet we get, but humans always seem to want to dry us off with a towel when we get home. Actually, we quite enjoy this as it's really a disguised cuddle, and we can't get enough of those.

Licking your human's ears not only promotes cleanliness but also expresses your affection. We learn about licking from our mums, who lick us to groom us. When we grow up we can clean ourselves although Zara is very good at looking after me like this.

How to help your humans around the house and garden

Of course if anything eatable drops on the floor we are always quick to help our humans by eating it up before they have to get up to fetch a cloth.

Occasionally we feel that the floor could do with an extra wash. Our technique for initiating this is to empty the bin at night - the mess is so tremendous that they have to clean the floor the next day!

Our humans don't really like this and so prevent us from getting into the bin by putting the stool in front of it...but sometimes they forget. Zara can pull open the drawer with her front paws to check what's inside. Sometimes the tastiest and messiest things are at the bottom.

If the bin is full, then this means emptying out the rest of the rubbish onto the floor. Sometimes we take the more interesting bits over to our beds for further inspection.

The only bad part is when a human discovers the mess in the morning...prepare to be shouted at. However, it's the only method we've come up with for keeping the kitchen floor clean, which is very important.

Zara is always interested in tasting what our humans have been eating. Wait for your human to stack the dishwasher, especially large plates with gravy and sauce. Then lick each plate as it goes in - after all, this contributes to the cleaning operation, which your human does not always understand.

Then when your human pushes the tray in, there is often a yummy titbit on the dishwasher door when it is flat but you need to be pretty quick before your human closes it. Another piece of advice to you other dogs - don't try eating the dishwasher tablet. Zara did this once and immediately regretted it!

Catching rabbits is a great way we help our humans with their gardening as the rabbits eat Jane's home-grown vegetables which is very annoying! We are the guards of the vegetable garden.

We also think digging holes is a great help for gardening. It moves the earth around, which is surely a good idea. However, our humans don't seem to appreciate this, especially when we dig out the same hole that they have just filled in.

How to apologise for occasional mistakes

We never make mistakes intentionally. Sometimes it just happens. We dogs like to please our humans as much as we can.

It's absolutely fine to chew bones, but it's not OK when our humans come down in the morning and find one of their favourite shoes chewed up. This probably happened some hours ago, so it comes as a bit of a surprise to us that they are so annoyed when they see the shoe, as we live in the present moment. Usually it's just one shoe chewed. The other shoe is fine, so why don't they focus on that one?

We can tell from their tone of voice that our humans are very annoyed with us (well, with

Zara, because she does most of the chewing although I must admit that I went through quite a few shoes when I was a puppy).

We make ourselves smaller, look down, bow our heads and slink into the corner with our tails between our legs and looking guilty. Most humans don't know that this is really a submission gesture showing that we know who is boss.

In our time, we have chewed through shoes, trainers (several pairs), wellies, bits of sofa, cushions, recipe books, pencils, and even parts of our own beds. Humans really should be more careful, and shouldn't leave things lying around the kitchen when they go to bed at night.

One day David bought Zara a really large chew that looked like a real bone. He said that it was meant to last three months. Not for Zara. She finished it off in one night, but she didn't feel very well in the morning…

If it looks like your human is going on a trip, get into the car to make sure you're not left behind. If they leave a window open you can just climb in. However, sometimes they think you're lost and start shouting frantically when you are actually in the car. This happened recently in Aldeburgh and everyone set off in all directions to look for me when I was in the car all the time!

As you know we like really rich smells, so if you can roll in it to get something on your collar, the smell can last all day. Sometimes there are other nice things to roll on like a dead seagull Zara saw recently on Elie beach or a dead sheep in Dumfries – although that time poor Zara was hosed down with very cold water. Our humans don't have the same refined sense of smell and can't seem to appreciate this.

Occasionally, we manage to escape, and sometimes we go off for several hours. The main thing is to keep an eye on your humans to make sure they don't see you sneaking off. You can pretend to be looking around in the garden, then suddenly you make off before they realise what has happened.

If they call us within five minutes, we always come back, but otherwise we are just too far away to hear them calling (well, not really, we can actually hear miles away). Then they just have to wait until we come back. Our humans are always glad - even relieved - to see us, asking us where on earth we have been.

We don't tell them, of course, but they can see from our noses that we've been digging some more holes. As long as these aren't in the garden, they don't mind unless we're so muddy that they need to hose us down. We don't really enjoy this either. Once Zara was so muddy that we hardly recognised her!

Very considerately, our humans leave the conservatory door open, and we'll be there in the morning. However, just recently a great escape went badly wrong. Our humans came back at midnight to find only Zara in the kitchen. We had escaped earlier in the afternoon when the delivery man left the door open.

I don't normally have any problems jumping right over fences in one go, but I got my front paw tangled up in some sheep wire and I couldn't move. I pulled and yelped but I had to spend a horrible night outside with my paw up above my head.

Luckily our local farmer had been mending a fence close by and heard me howling. He

thought I was a fox but realised it must have been me when he heard I was missing in the morning, which was very lucky.

I was about a mile away, up on the hill but Jane found me straight away because our farmer had told us where the noises had come from. She cut me free and she and Charlotte carried me down the hill to the car. Charlotte stayed in the boot with me all the way to the vet. They both looked like war heroes, covered in blood, when we arrived!

We went straight to the vet and I was put to sleep while they did X-rays and stitched up my leg. When I came out they put a lampshade on my head to stop me from unpicking the stitches. You can't imagine how irritating this was, especially as I kept on bumping into things and couldn't lick my wound. And it was very hard getting through fences. I'm glad to say I'm

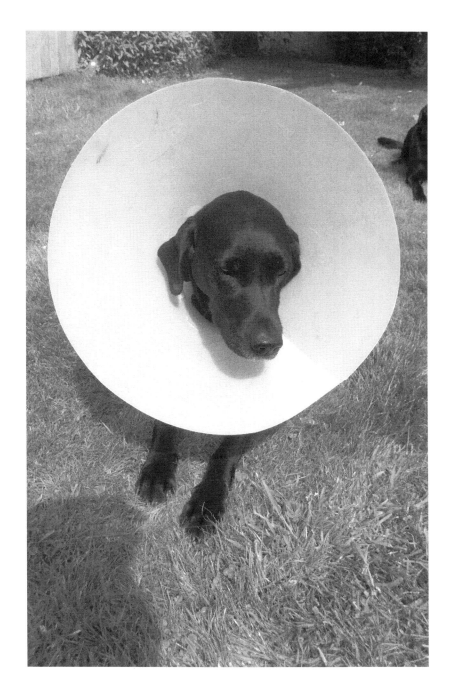

fine now and just to make sure I jumped over a 5-foot-6 wall several times in Glen Lyon.

Zara has been lucky so far as the worst thing that has happened to her - twice would you believe - is getting a stick stuck across the roof of her mouth, which doesn't improve the quality of her breath...

How to pose for photos

Looking at photos makes humans happy – especially when they are of us dogs! They love to put photos of us in frames around the house or post photos of us in photo apps.

You have to make sure that they show you from your best side so it's very important to know how to pose for photographs. The first thing is to learn how to sit still and look attentive (Zara is exceptional at this and makes me very proud.) If your human is taking your photograph they get very annoyed if you get up and move around unless they are taking a video.

Group photos can be tricky. The other dogs may not be as adept at posing as you are, or worse still their humans can spend ages fiddling with their hair and changing where they are standing! This can be very trying, but patience is a virtue.

Every situation can turn into a photo opportunity, so always be on the lookout and check your social media regularly to make sure they haven't posted any embarrassing photos.

We'd love to hear about your adventures and tips for looking after your humans. We hope you've found our tips useful. You can share your own advice through our social media – look out for us!

In the meantime just remember that your stressed-out humans need your care and affection more than ever.